Hooked on You

Joseph Mangraviti

PublishAmerica
Baltimore

First printing

PublishAmerica has allowed this work to remain exactly as the author intended, verbatim, without editorial input.

ISBN: 1-60672-736-2
PUBLISHED BY PUBLISHAMERICA, LLLP
www.publishamerica.com
Baltimore

Printed in the United States of America

To my wonderful wife Diane and to my great kids, David, Mark and Daniel

Introduction

The poems in *Hooked on You* are meant to express feelings about loving and living life to its fullness: romance, family, friends, hopes, dreams and also God. I feel the enigmatic magic and power of poetry in creating a mood, in captivating and exalting feelings, and in experiencing empathy. I see poetry as a way to find a little bit of heaven on a sunny day when you are sitting on a cliff. You are overlooking the ocean. You are happy you are alive. You feel in your heart you are part of the vast universe. On a rainy day, you may find yourself indoors having a conversation. The words cause a smile. The smile leads to a hug. The hug makes two become one in expressing love and in the creation of life. When the day is dark, you feel what others experience: the struggles of a rebellious soul facing problems and sometimes, unfortunately, adversities. Let your lust for life become your everyday poetry.

CONTENTS

Tormented Ecstasy

Real Dreams

Fair of Tales

Fiber of Manhood

Body and Soul

Exploring the Past

State of Sin

Funky Therapy

Home Joys

Living the Love

The Triumph of Love

Love—always triumphant
Reigns in your heart
Hopes and dreams

When a kiss on her hand
Is followed by a kiss on her lips—
Your heart palpitates with joy
Your mind is dazzled by her beauty
Your soul feels a subtle magic
Your body becomes enchanted

When you hold her tight—
You feel her heart beats frantically
You see her lips coming closer
You sense her embrace asking for more
You are the King of the Earth
She is the Queen of the Sky

When the two of you become one flesh—
The ocean glows under a splendid sun
The earth trembles with excitement
The sky salutes you with rainbows
Heaven pours down its blessings
Because Love
Once again
Has triumphed
Over loneliness and misery!

The Look of Love

The look of love is in your eyes
Your heart jumps and your mouth mumbles
The moon and the sun light your path
Your smile glows with happiness

The look of love is on your lips
Your lips open for the feeding of your soul
The softness of your lips leads to magic
Past, present and future merge swiftly
Into a kiss of endless love

The look of love is in your touch
You are burning with lust and desire
You feel the frenzy and the rush
Your heart beats to a vibrant new rhythm

The look of love is on your mind
You cannot wait to hold, hug and kiss
Your mind is dazzled and your heart is mystified
Your soul sings songs of enchantment

The look of love is in your heart
You experience indescribable wonders
Your excitement cannot be contained
Happiness resides in your heart at last

That Madly in Love Feeling

A holy temple is in your soul—gentle and fair.
You save it for me and for my own pleasure.
Your intimate and secret desires reside there.
What you hold deeply, for you I also treasure.

I knew you would always be mine, Pumpkin Pie.
The first embrace sealed our fate in Love's bounds.
You spread your wings and flew beyond the sky,
Fireworks lit my soul with bewildering sounds.

Even when I sleep, I dream of you fervently.
Away, I crave you with desire and passion.
I spend all day long missing you painfully.

I can't get enough of you, Diane, in any fashion,
You are the full moon, white and bright,
And intriguing as the twinkling stars at night.

Let Love Lead the Way!

Let Love lead you away from loneliness!
Enchant your days with true happiness!
Tell bravely that true love is what you seek.

Lately you have been walking in the dark
Over the clouds and down all the Earth.
Vehemently searching for a soul mate:
Eternal quest to fulfill your destiny

Longing every day for that special someone,
Empowered by dreams and fantasies,
Awaiting for you are hugs and kisses.
Desire and Love to enrich your life!

Tenderness, caring and friendship
Has Fate in store for you—to last a lifetime,
Entangled you shall be in each other's arms.

Wait not, but swim in the deep sea of Love
And believe in your fantasies and dreams!
Yes, hurry before the day quickly awakens!

How Do You Tell Her?

How do you tell her—
You are in ecstasy when she appears
You want more than a kiss and a hug
You wish to hold her tight
To feel her heartbeat
   It's like you're in heaven
   When you two are one flesh
How do you tell her—
You want to share
Your soul
By being inside her
 And to be part of God's creation

How do you tell her—
You will buy her a ring
Which won't be five carats
But your love is worth
More
Than all the diamonds
In the world

Just be yourself, Big Guy!
Speak with your heart
And deceive her not!

Irresistible!

Beautiful
More beautiful than ever
The most beautiful!

Lovely
Stunning
Exotic
Breathtaking!
Enchanting
Alluring
Yet mysterious!

You are an inspiration!
You are endless springtime
You are the lovely Queen of Hearts
You are an enchantress!

Anything you wear seems worth millions
Anything you say is music and poetry
Grace, poise and charm fill the air when you dance

At night, you become Sleeping Beauty
Eagerly waiting for Prince Charming
To wake you up in the morning
With Love's first kiss

Never Say "No" to Love

Never should you say "No" to Love:
Eternal desire of a benign fate,
Virtue of unleashed lust,
Endless longing by a tormented heart,
Restless search of a soul mate,

Silent keep your lips and hopes;
And when magic comes along,
Yeager embrace your destiny.

Never knowing how and where you will go,
On sight bright, your eyes shall meet.

Turning and shaping brand new futures,
Open to hope once ailed by loneliness.

Love is for tomorrow—hope is for today.
Open your arms and smile to Love.
Visited by Lady Luck, in dreams to be fulfilled
End a search driven by your innate passion.

For the Love of Her People

Lady Godiva
1040>1080

After she accepted her husband's dare.
There she was—unclothed and fair!
To feed her people, the Earl's bride
Bravely swallowed her pride.

To spare a tax increase, she rode her horse—
Naked, hair down and no remorse.
The Coventry good folks felt obliged
To turn their back or hide

History recorded her memorable ride
Because she made a stride.
Nothing would be the same thereof:
Her triumph—result of altruistic love!

So far where too far can't be reached
A gentle soul had preached.
The Earl's egoism and impetuosity
Diffused by his bride's intrepidity.

The Light

Then God said, "Let it be Light";
And there was Light! (Gen 1.3)
Look at the universe unfurled.
See Love permeating the world.

Feel it in your mind and soul.
Feel it in your heart.
Let it happen and let it roll!
Let it set you apart!

You were conceived in love
So in return you can love.
Let it in your heart burn.
Never expect a thing in return.

You were born to give freely,
To charm, enchant and dazzle.
You have the Light really
To see God's face and not be baffled.

When you see a star twinkling,
It's God's eye blinking.
He says, "Don't be beguiled!
I love you, Sweet Child"

Arts of Seduction

After Dark

Don Juan in Love

Below your window I'll be at midnight—
When all will be still—no sound, no light.
I will crawl quietly into your own room
Eagerly to play at last the passionate groom

I can't wait, Milady, to make you mine
Nor wait to have your mind completely blown.
I badly need to see you in the dark—shine
And wait to hear you sweetly moan.

I want you! I need you desperately! You I desire!
Let's drive our passion, higher, higher and higher!
I want to see you burn by my blazing fire!

Let's our lust the romance continue to ignite
You'll be the lady; I'll be the brave knight.
Milady, let's make hot love this very night!

I Want You

Casanova in Love

I want to embrace you tight for hours.
I want to hold you close to my heart.
I need to feel your heartbeat
Beating frantically.
You can feel mine pulsating madly.
I must explore and massage
Every inch of your body.
Just hugging and kissing your lips gently
Is all I desire.
You belong to me! You sense it! You know it!
It feels right! It feels great!
Destiny has brought us together
To be one flesh.
Lasting skintight hugs will lead us
To heavenly delights:
Pleasures of the flesh
And pleasures of the mind.
I am going crazy over you.
You are the most desirable!
I cannot endure the torment
To love you from a distance.
I want to feel your body trembling with pleasure.
I must have you at any cost
Else I will die in terrible pains.
I need to hold you and make you mine constantly.
I want you every hour of every day
Of every year, Milady!
From a delicate and innocent kiss
To passionate ecstasy,
From quiet lovemaking
To voluptuous and explosive rapture,
From lustful moments to an inescapable frenzy,
I must explore your mind

And deeply penetrate your very soul,
So we both can explode in fireworks
On a bed of earthquakes

If You Were Mine

Tristan's Pledge

If you were mine—
I would turn the clock back to your teens
The years when your heart palpitated frantically
At the sweet anticipation
Of Love's first kiss and embrace.
If you were mine—
I would have you close your beautiful eyes
Have you dream a fantasy
I would turn into reality
I would hug you, kiss you and possess you!

If you were mine—
I would cast away any inhibitions you have.
I would bring to surface
Your deepest desires

If you were mine—
I would massage your mind
And feed your soul
I would appreciate your body
As the greatest gift of all!
I would not stop loving you
Until your moans reached heaven

If you were mine
I would worship you
Every day
And every night
For times to come!

Dance for Me, Salome!

The King's Proposal

Music, dance and lustful eyes!
Courtship, promises and secret plans!
The birds are busy singing joyously
For your pleasure.
The bees are making honey
To nourish your very soul.
Music plays you like an instrument.
You are enchanting!
You are divinely beautiful!
Dancing helps you express your desires,
Hidden in your heart.
Love is all around you: passion and ecstasy.
Your lustful eyes open the gate
Of the magical Garden of Delights.
My amorous and desirous eyes
Wish to undress you stuck naked.
My expert hands want to massage you
Into an endless sweet rapture.
Let destiny unfolds!
Let nature unravels the lust bottled in.
Let the art of lovemaking
Become the heavenly breath of life.
Smile at love and fulfill dreams
You didn't even know you had.
Spread your wings, Babe, and fly.
Fly, Babe, fly!

The True Meaning of Romance

John the Baptist

Sing and dance, Salome!
Sing and dance until dawn
Shake things up with love songs
Let the lonely believe in magic again
Perform the Dance of the Seven Veils
Long forgotten
       Yet fulfilling, rich and rewarding

As the hands hold
The lips touch in dreams
To come true real soon
When music is divine
It is pure pleasure
To the ear, mind and soul
Two minds explore the challenge
To stretch limits to fly beyond the sky
Two hearts palpitate as one
Before the eyes of a loving God
Two bodies become one flesh
In the miracle of creation

What's the true meaning of romance?
Happiness and pleasures—
Finally you hear simple sweet words
That melts your very soul
You see yourself spreading your wings
To fly to touch heaven
Your heart is filled with
Songs
Dances
And the enigmatic magic of poetry
You smell the flowers of your kisses
Growing all around you

You taste the wine
In the cup of eternal springtime
Enriched by true love

Dance of the Seven Veils

Salome
(Mat 14)

With only seven veils dressed
Salome entered the hall
By music erotically possessed
Danced the king to enthrall

The audience was greatly impressed.
Off with the veil of humility.
Women got jealous, men excited:
Down the veil of domesticity!

The eyes were fixed and fascinated.
Down the veil of abstinence!
With desire and longing sighted
Off with the veil of temperance.

The king his lust felt to reveal
Down the veil of innocence!
Fell the veil of impetuous zeal
Off with the veil of purity.

Shocked was the community
By her mother's request.
John lost his head
While Salome's heart bled.

The Genie

I'm the genie who, in a magic lamp, resides.
I'm here to fulfill your most intimate dreams.
I take you on a journey of self-discovery, besides.
It's a wonderland where imagination streams.

Why do you settle for simple pleasures?
I can provide you with ecstasy and bliss.
Open the door to my world of treasures.
It's the wisdom you don't want to miss.

Learn all you can achieve to set you apart.
Make a wish! Wish for Love or for Glory.
The best wishes are those of a dear heart.

You can write a new and exciting life story.
Indulge in the pleasures that lead to passion.
Make a wish! Show yourself some compassion.

Tempting an Angel

A Gigolo at Work

Wrap me up with sweet kisses.
Let me be your birthday present!
Then un-wrap me when nobody is around.
You were staring at me on the dance floor.
You liked what you saw and you want more—
The smile of a celebrity I shine with.
The demeanor of royalty you admire,
The mind of a harlot for your pleasure,
The soul of an experienced
And real man you crave.
I am the genie who lives in the magic lamp.
I can give you all you want
And dream about.
No limits! No inhibitions! No thinking!
You know it! You want to be bad!
You want it all!
You wonder if I make
The perfect husband for you:
All day and night spent together,
Always making out
While responsibilities and chores
Become a distant memory.

Do you want love that lasts forever?
Do you want fun that lasts forever, instead?
You decide!
You can take all the time you need.
I am here for you
And I am waiting patiently.
I am also very real
And I live in your fantasies as well.

Queen of Seduction

Cleopatra
69-30 B.C.

As the Persian carpet
Unrolled before Caesar's eyes
There she was, Cleopatra!
A queen of glamour
A queen of beauty
A queen of love
A queen of wisdom
The Queen of the Nile
    The Queen of Kings

The winds of seduction
Inflamed Caesar
And he fathered her child
Restored to her throne
As the rightful monarch
She fed Caesar
Pleasures of the flesh
And pleasures of the palate

After Murder swept away her Love
She inflamed a new one—Mark Anthony
She charmed and fascinated him
Once he went black
    To his old ways, he couldn't go back
She made him husband and father
She turned him into a god
And he turned her into a goddess

With destiny and Rome unkind
She had the asp kiss her goodbye

The Greatest Lover

Giacomo Casanova
1725-1798

A Venetian gentleman
A preacher
An entrepreneur
A philosopher
An alchemist
A poet and an author
An occultist
A world traveler like no other!

But most of all
He was
The greatest lover
The world has ever known!

He was a well-mannered heartthrob
   Gifted with exquisite persistence
      He had the ladies smile and also sob
While he practiced the art of patience

He voiced his feelings of—
Love and attraction
Praise and appreciation
To the rationale he appealed
   To the ladies his longing he revealed

He could not resist women
   And they could not resist him

Hollywood Heartthrob

Rudolph Valentino
1895-1926

Came to the States for bread, butter and cream
Chasing, like all, the American dream
And in Hollywood stardom he reigned supreme

Italian gigolo at first
Then talented Tango dancer
Until the movies became his answer
He portrayed
A matador, a sheik and a horseman
     In self-confidence blooming
         With chivalry and awareness
    In fashion and perfect grooming
With machismo and tenderness

To the women in the theaters
He made ecstatic love
    Some killed themselves
When he closed his eyes
Under the powder puff
Perceived
As the most romantic movie star
And the most desirable man
To duels he challenged and dared
And to boxing matches
He had them scared

Always living on the edge—
Excitement
Fame
Scandals
Broke
The heart of the Heartbreaker

Pleasures of the Flesh

Pleasures

My pleasures are—
To look at your enchanting smile, Diane,
To hear your sweet talk of unspoken thoughts
To smell the perfume coming from your heart
To taste the beauty of your gentle soul
To inflame your heart and mind
With my endless love

When the senses highlight pleasure
Love highlights life
That's the simplicity in loving
And being loved in return

Heaven can be found on earth—
When two souls seeking each other
Find each other
When two hearts meant to be together
Stick together
When all that is beautiful and holy
Is right at home worth waiting for
And not everywhere
In the Land of Nowhere

Magic Dust

Heaven on my planet
Is the hug that lasts a lifetime.
It's the kiss between two naked souls
Who realize what they only possess
Is the moment.

As hands touch more and more franticly,
Fate unfolds while embraces turn into frenzy.
A frenzy driven
By passion and lust for life.

Heavy breathing becomes
Uncontrollable moaning.
Longing for more seems
A dream impossible to fulfill.
Only then,
Poetry leads to magic
And magic to ecstasy.

Love Is Forever

Love is forever and ever.
Open your heart and sweet soul.
Visit the depth of your own craving,
Endlessly burning inside.

Inside, you find romance and magic
Sweetly nurtured by the love you feel.

Fill your heart with love songs,
Over the rainbow and beyond.
Exquisite is your heavenly smile.
Velvet, satin and softness is your skin!
Experience the depth of your very soul.
Rest and dream; dream and love.

Love Rewards Those Who Wait

The Knight's Love Song

Love rewards those who wait.
Oh, Milady! In time we shall be together!
Velvet, satin and real lust will surround us.
Ecstasy will be the passion driven by our embraces.

Rest assured of my deep love for you.
Enter the bedroom with dreams and desires.
Waiting there for you is sweet tenderness,
Absolutely pure passion to consume us both.
Rest by me, play with me, my magical fair lady.
Destined we have been to experience love's pleasures .
Swim in the sea of enchantments and delights.

Transcendental in dreams and fantasies,
Hold you dear and close to my inner self.
Open your heart and arms for me!
Sweetly fulfill those dreams we both have.
Entered you have the chamber of my heart.

Who waits will cherish unforgettable moments,
Holding inside a magical bottled passion
Of everlasting and fulfilling love.

Who with wit and dedication conquers hearts,
Always collects the reward of one's labor.
Interestingly enough, such a person has magic,
Tranquility, serenity and plenty of love to share.

My One and Only

The Court Jester's Song

Mine to keep and to cherish you are.
Yes, to cherish and to love, Milady.

Over the rainbow and the clouds
Not once, but for a lifetime
Enter my own Garden of Eden.

Alleluia, found at last, it's ecstasy!
Nurtured by one's hopes and wishes,
Down and out with perfidious loneliness!

On eagle's wings we fly to reach heaven,
Nested in passion and in ecstasy,
Long last rapture for the pure hearts.
Yes, happiness has been found at last!

Rush into My Arms, Isolde!

Tristan's Love Call

Rush into my arms, Sweet Isolde!
Undeniably desired by words never spoken,
Surrender I encourage you, to true passion.
Hail, Isolde, Queen of Hearts!

Invented you have been by a long wait,
Never knowing when it would happen,
Territory unexplored ever before.
Oh, yes, I want you more than I can say.

Marry me at dawn when the sun awakes
Yielding Love's Labor and reward.

Anticipating the most exquisite sensations,
Restlessly longing for one's sacred love,
Midnight is for eternal lovemaking—
Silence, interrupted only by whispers.

Before you came to make me shine
And to save me from desolation,
Beautiful, I saw you in my dreams—
Everlasting romance before moonlight.

Hanky Panky

The King and the Lady-in-Waiting

Resting next to each other after a sunny day,
Intertwined in a hug of insatiable lust,
Serenaded by birds' love songs,
Kept we are indoors by the need of each other.
Yeager we seem to explore our secret fantasies.

Resting assured of the promise of a true love,
Enter we have the secret chamber of pure lust.
Never question each other's feelings.
Desire we discover is the answer to prayers.
Entertained by the magic of the moment
Victorious over boredom and loneliness
Outcast by a judgmental society
Undertaking risks bigger than us
Surrendered we have to a force bigger than us.

Flames

Flames constantly burn inside you feverishly.
Real fire, pristine lust, uncontrollable passion!
As the flames consume your inner-self deeply,
Your heart and soul seek absolute gratification.

Charm, driven by fate, glows on you brightly.
The flame of life burns your soul constantly.
The flame of lust fires up your heart mystically.
The flame of adventure reigns inside anxiously.

Explore your boundaries, by lust possessed,
By stretching your limits—your ultimate quest.
Nature has again let the winds of passion blow.

Share your mind and soul with a precious kiss:
A kiss expressing the promise of a kind tomorrow
By living the present in bursting delightful bliss.

A Gigolo's Memoirs

Wednesday night was Ladies' Night at the club—
The cheers and the noise of tipsy women
Whose dreams
Were limited only by the size
Of their pocketbook

The white of the tuxedo, shirt, bowtie and shoes
Made Mr. Continental look sleek and sharp.
As the beat of music got louder and louder
They refreshed the drinks,
And the face with powder.

As the jacket, the shirt and the pants came off
Singles, tens and twenties
In the bikini went in.
Were they cheering at the flashy clothes?
Were they seduced
By his pure and sensitive heart?
Were the sleek dance steps the answer?
Whatever it was, they were drooling
Over the hot blooded dancer!

It was the follies of youth
And the age of fig leaves bliss.
It was a time
Spent on the pursuit of happiness,
Looking for paradise
In all wrong places.

Nature's Call

The lion wakes up—feeling his need to mate:
The need to answer Mother Nature's call
He let out snarls, he roars; his mood is great.
Toward him, the lioness is starting to crawl.

She's overwhelmed with desire to surrender.
She's the mate of the jungle's potent king.
He mounts her; she's the gentle female gender.
She squirms, twists, and makes her head swing.

He massages and licks her neck endlessly.
He bites her neck to keep her in place.
His needs make him go inside repetitively.

More snarls! Against her neck, he rubs his face
Until all he got is inside her—in full deposited.
Now he lies down under the sun—frazzled.

Tormented Ecstasy

Unreturned Love

King Arthur

My happiness is seeing you being you.
I love to watch you, Genevieve,
Do what you do, always with ease.
You wear the most charming smile.
You make everything
Look wonderful and fantastic.
It is eternal springtime out there
When you are around.
The birds sing, the bees make honey
And the flowers bloom.

You are truly one of the nicest, finest
And greatest people.
The world is a better place
Because of your presence.
The magic of your smile becomes poetry,
Poetry that transports me
Into a world of ecstasy.
As I close my eyes and I am loving you,
Touching every inch of your body,
Giving you happiness
The only way I know how—
Pleasure and passion.

Thank you for letting me experience
All the terrific feelings
You have easily been able
To bring out in me.
May God bless you for igniting
That magic flame in my heart,
Long time ago extinguished
By the hardship and the anguish
Life has pierced my heart.
You will never know

How much I truly care for you.
You haven't taken the time yet
To show me you care for me, too.
For the first time in my life,
I realize love can hurt badly.
It is sinful you ignore
A love-burning heart
That beats for you.

Heaven and Hell

Sir Lancelot

When I close my eyes
I feel you, Genevieve, next to me

I discover I am in heaven
Because heaven
Is being in each other's arms
Loving and living

You make me feel
I am the instrument
That turns your empty days
Into happy ones
I love to see you
Finding in me all you need:
Hugs and kisses
That last a lifetime

I cannot get enough of you
No matter how much I try!
The more you smile
The more I want you
The more you embrace me
The happier I become
The more you touch me
The more I want to be in you
You have special ways
To make me feel
You truly need me

I find impossible
To express
What you mean to me!
You are—
The sun

The moon
The sky
My very link to God!
You are ten heavens
Melted
Into one beautiful paradise

You are the answer
To prayers
I never knew
I had recited
You are—
All I want
All I need
My very reason for living
It's a miracle!

As I open my eyes
I watch
My heaven turn into hell
You are not there!
Even worse—
You will never be mine!
We have been played
By a cruel and unmerciful fate!

Impossible Dream

Tristan

Constantly thinking of you, Isolde,
Haunted I am by you day and night.
Always wrestles I find myself.
Set on fire by the flames of your love
In the treacherous quest
Of my impossible dream.
Never sleep, never rest and hardly eat.
Graceless I am abandoned to my sad fate.
Inside you I find real love and passion,
Magnetic pull on my lonely heart.
Open the door of my silent jail.
Shake it, break it and set me free.
Surely you feel my pain and sorrow.
In the depth of the night I am lost!
Bravely accepting the slavery of my heart,
Longing, as always I am
For the magic of your kisses.
Eager to see your dazzling smile,
Dreaming how lovely you are I am,
Resting your head on my chest,
Embracing all night until the break of dawn.
Anticipation sizzles about the day we meet again.
Meet we shall at the end of the Earth.
So, for now, let sunset lead us to sunshine.

Missing You, Dad!

You're my dear dad who, due to a cancer blow,
I was not lucky to love and to get to know—
You're far away in heaven
Where I cannot see you again

Your death left me virtually devastated
Part of me died with you surely
After all these years gone and hated
I still find your loss unbearable

My soccer games you didn't attend
Where I loved to compete and contend
You didn't take me hunting, fishing
Mountain climbing or outdoor camping
My school teachers you didn't meet
To learn how I did in the classes' elite
A spruce with me you didn't cut down
As our Christmas tree to be the best in town
You were not there for me, your lad
When I was in trouble sick, or sad
You didn't walk with mom into the hall
On my wedding day to smile and stand tall

I had to be the man
With no man around
To teach me how to be one
No boy deserves to be bound
To such tough challenges' cruel gun

My tormented ecstasy on Father's Day—
I smile to my kids and a happy image I portray
With no dad of mine to see grow old and gray

Why did you have to die?
I was only four years old—
Definitely too young to cry

When I look up at the sky at night
I see a beautiful star glowing bright
I know you are that star
Letting me know from afar
Watching over me—you are
That's when I strongly feel
Your love for me is very real—
Father's and son's enduring seal!

Though I will always be the boy
Whose love for you is my sad joy
The time has come for me
To say "Goodbye"
Finally your death I have accepted!
I will go on proud with my life
Be the man—to be I was destined
Enjoying the happiness I deserve

My Dream of Grandma

I was swimming,
On a sunny day—summer's celebration.
In my teens enjoying
The sea and the beach—God's creation.
To my own surprise and delight,
Nobody was at the beach on sight.
Suddenly the water became rough.
Thunder, lightening and rain were tough.
I did my best to swim to shore, but I could not.
I was afraid to drawn, being in a storm caught.

I saw a distant rowboat with a tiny light
Coming toward me as to tame my fright.
You, Grandma, were standing on it, concerned,
In order to rescue me, very determined—
Your first grandchild of your first-born son.
You pulled me out of the water,
Sat me safely on the boat, danger to shun.
Brought me to shore and let me off later.
I didn't want, Grandma, to get off and depart.
I wanted to spend time with you.
I wanted to tell you badly with all my heart
How much I love and miss you.
For long, you had been in the heavenly skies.
You smiled at me with deep love in your eyes.
Into the distant horizon your boat back went
The way it had come, in spite of my lament.

Grandma, you came to warn me in my dream
Of the rough waters coming later in my life.
My mind and soul slipped into an extreme regime
Only for me to wake up in sorrow and strife.

Please, forgive me, Grandma! I miserably failed.
Pray God on my behalf for the way I derailed.
The love that unconditionally binds us is brave
And goes on beyond the sadness of the grave.

Sorry!

How do you say you're sorry
When being sorry is not enough?

How do you explain
Self-deception?
How can you answer
For spiritual lethargy?
How do you deal
With serious problems
That won't go away?

Can you close your eyes
If you know
The door to hell may open—
To suck you in,
And to make you to fight
Your inner demons?

A time may come in your life
For your faith to be tested.
It's a time when beliefs and values
Seem to come crumbling down.

They say the answer can be found
In one's heart
If one looks deeply.
What do you do
When you look into your heart,
But there is no answer,
Only anguish?

You can have
Anything you want,
But the forbidden fruit.

What do you do
When what's forbidden
    Doesn't seem forbidden anymore?

The biggest fool is
The one who fools himself.
Are you a fool
When you crush
Under the weight
Of your problems?

What happens
If delivery from evil stops?
What do you do
When Evil
Stares right at you?

May God
Have infinite mercy on you,
My friend,
Because nobody else will!

Eclipse

A second time Grief visited my heart
When mom into the sunset had to depart:
A pervasive sense of loss and distress
Painted my days deep black, I confess.
Sorrow and suffering held me closely tight
To have me stubbed everywhere in fright.

Feelings of guilt and denial had me realize
I had been intensely beaten—and my cries
Into a dark dungeon kept my soul in ties.
A feeble light slowly came in. My jail got bright
When mom and dad as two angels came on site.
They were fine and wanted me to see the light.

They promised to come back one day to hold my hand
In crossing to the other side and in bliss—stand.
They smiled and helped me open my jail door
So I could walk away from my sorry plight.
Then home I ran, the magic castle I adore
To rebuild what Grief had ruined in its flight.

Eve's Fall

You can have all you want
But the forbidden fruit.
If you taste, you'll grow taunt
And pain shall be acute.

Your soul the Serpent will claim.
All generations to come
Shall you harshly blame.
To despair you'll succumb.

On the fruit, your heart is set.
It's deliciously appealing.
You think it's no threat:
Your hands over it—feeling.

You think you must taste it
You bite it anxiously.
You should've wasted it.
Now you withdraw suspiciously.

You discover you're destitute!
Seduction has you claimed.
You should've been astute.
Now you feel ashamed!

Letter to God

Dear Lord:

It seemed a day
Like any day that summer—warm and scented
I was in my teens
When, upon me, Your love lavishly descended
I felt the need
To offer You
My only possession—my heart
The secret place where, though apart,
My past, present and future coexist
That day—
I asked you to feed—
My whole heart, body and soul
I begged you, me to lead
And every day of my life to patrol
You accepted my gift—
Your love has poured over me ever since

Always, Your presence I feel
From me, a lot You seem to expect
You test my honesty for real
When I fault, You come to correct
Any false beliefs You repeal

At times, all the struggles
Make me feel overwhelmed—
As if to the cross I'm getting nailed

Dear God
To understand your ways, help me
        Over me, let Your mercy flow free!

Your lowly servant

Real Dreams

Changing Your Stars

You can change your stars.
To dream yourself—treat.
Listen to your heart by far;
Then follow your feet.

It' not where you're going,
But where—knowing.
A dream is no longer a dream
If you have a gleam.

Believe firmly; act accordingly.
Know it in your heart.
Love doing it enthusiastically.
Act suitably is the art!

Bravery is the path leading,
Even if a bit coarse.
That's goal achieving!
And Faith is the force!

Bonding

When waiting and longing are agonizing
When a sigh is more than a sigh softly
When lips touch gently and trembling
When hands feel you all over hungrily

When craving drives lustfully and madly
When love and lust express affection
When fantasies are delivered alluringly
When by not being perfect is perfection

When pleasure can't even be preached
And going too far cannot be reached
When making out is the holy connection

When two, nature's call, are answering
And reaching heaven is the direction
It is more than passion, it is bonding!

The American Dream

You certainly have food on your kitchen table
And a roof over a smart head—very capable!
A great business, a family, friends and esteem!
You, Champ, have realized the American dream.

The time has come for you to reach beyond,
Beyond the dream, so to stardom you can bond.
Let your skills, talents and capabilities shine.
Bring heaven down to earth by attentive design.

You make a delicious sauce and also fine wine.
Hunting, fishing and sports are daringly divine.
Now cross the ocean, fly the air; just don't quit!

Listen to your call: embrace life opportunities!
Be all you can be: to fine goals yourself commit.
Spread your wings and fly high beyond the skies.

Best Friends

Best friends
   And soul mates
   You two shall be!
Enter, without fear,
   The magical Garden of Eden,
Silently
   To taste and enjoy
   The forbidden fruit,
To share a bed of dreams,
   Which will end loneliness.

Feast marries Desire
   When two hearts
   Find each other,
Restlessly, eagerly,
   Anxiously and feverishly,
Interested always
   In the mysteries of the night.
Exquisite you shall find
   The humble kisses of true love.
Nothing but romance,
   Remember,
   Can bring out a rainbow.
Delightfully
   You shall dance
   In the Fountain of Youth!
Shortly,
   The Fountain will turn
   Into a sea of endless Love.

Seasons of a Dream

A brave page had a dream—
With passion, to explore
      To conquer at any extreme
           True love, to discover
The brave page achieved his dream

Galloped in, a black knight—
    He turned into a man the boy
        And the page into a white knight
But he destroyed what the boy,
Now a man, had achieved with delight

The white knight had a dream—
With passion, to explore
      To conquer at any extreme
           True love, to discover
The white knight achieved his dream

Again, the black knight
Galloped in with his lance
Firmly, the white knight
Charged in and took his chance

Who Is Jean?

Jean is the home humble goddess
Jean is the steady friend when you have none
Jean is the angel and the sweet lady we all love
Jean is not a name anymore
Because worn with so much splendor

Jean is here to make reality out of dreams
And dreams out of everyday events
God bless our Jean!
May He preserve her in faith and in health
Jean forever and forever Jean!

Sunshine

Whisper into my ear, oh Sunshine!
Whisper into my hopes and dreams
Bright as bright you can be
Sunshine at last I want to see
To have and to have not
To hold a dream
Of sunny days to come

Colors of the Rainbow

The magic of the rainbow, a stairway to heaven,
Covenant between man and God, excites my soul.
In a thanksgiving prayer, heart-felt and proven
I'm the lucky part and you, Diane—the whole.

Peace and tranquility have gently dwelled in my heart
Since I met you, my body has been swinging in voracity.
Wisdom and virtue teach the need never to be apart.
Enthusiasm, energy and **passion** bind us in simplicity.

We find the way to **explore**. By love consumed,
Spring we become: we **grow**, bud and bloom.
We look up to appreciate **infinity**, never to assume,
While possibilities all around us—accessible seem.
At night, in each other's arms, **serenity** reigns supreme.

Good News

No news is good news!
Good news is made
By ideas that have succeeded
Success is the color of a happy life
A happy life is for happy souls
A happy soul
Always
Delivers good news
And so are you—Dear Lady
You're the good news!

Thanks!

When saying "Thanks" is hardly enough
But enough to show appreciation
When appreciation is hardly enough
But enough to glow on one's smile
When one's smile candidly says it all
Then saying "Thanks" is the sunrise
And "You're welcome" is the sunset

The Fairest of Them All

Lina Cavalieri

1874-1944

The most beautiful woman in the world!
The soprano voice of a siren—
She had the audience swirl and twirl

Orphaned at fifteen—
In a convent bound
Raised by zealous nuns
The theater, she found
And had success in tons

A gifted and spectacular performer
     She dazzled and charmed
As the hearts for her got warmer
Married a few Princes Charming

The poise of a glamour queen
The soul of a temptress
A womanhood fortress
An Italian Love Goddess!

A volunteer nurse in World War II—
Devotedly alert
The sick and hurt
Helping and soothing
To her God, during a bombing
She gave up her soul
While on a peaceful stroll.

Queen of Hearts

Happy Birthday
And the very best!
Absolutely stunning
And sizzling, you are!
Pleasing, you are to the eyes,
To the mind and to the heart:
 Permanent seal
 Of long lasting love
 And friendship.
Definitely you deserve
A very Happy Birthday!

Bestowed upon you
Is a gentle and sweet soul.
Candy, spice and everything nice
You are made of.
Heat and magic, possessed by you,
Touch lonely hearts.

Destined you have been
Since the beginning of time
To shine like
A magnificent star,
Aphrodite herself,
Alluring and seductive you are!

Yeager and determined,
You pride yourself
To make eyes sparkle.
Charmingly dear, you become
The Muse of Inspiration.
You open doors
To forbidden rituals of passion.

Assured be your compassion and love
Lead to heaven.
Radiant in the glow of an innocent kiss,
Forever you dazzle brightly.

Knight of Spades

What can I wish a guy that has it all?
You have—
The smile of a movie star
The demeanor of a king
The soul of a real man
The noble heart of a knight

Yours are—
The love of family, friends and co-workers
The innate skills to reach for the stars
The potential to go so far
Where too far
Cannot be reached

What personal traits
Do I see dwelling within you?
The energy you feel
The passion for life you possess
The innate but elusive desire
To have the cake and eat it too

Let the metaphysical wisdom—
To understand the human heart
The enigmatic mind and soul
Of the people around you
Enrich devotion to your mission in life
So your name can live on
Walk tall on the road of life
A life made of simple pleasures
That excites the mind
To formulate challenging goals
Goals become
Remarkable achievements
And unforgettable memories

Perfect you are for being delightfully human
Human you are for being perfectly special
You are the man!
Happy Birthday, Big Guy!

Fair of Tales

A Tale of Passion

How much love
May a princess and her prince share?
How much is true romance
Important in lovemaking?
How much is commitment sealing
The hearts of two soul mates?
Sweet Sleeping Beauty asks
Herself these questions
In her long sleep
Caused by the evil fairy's spell

For now she can only wait and dream
Of her dashing and daring prince
The prince's kiss of true love
Will break the spell and mark
The beginning of an endless romance:
Rich, passionate and fulfilling
Finally the love of a real man!
She wants him next to her—
Grabbing her all over
Kissing her
And penetrating
Her very soul with brute force
Have him mark her
As his woman
His property
And his queen
Have him seed her
With his male gift
Driven by his overwhelming needs
Have him worship her beauty
While she worships him
On her knees like a god
He is a god of raw potency

Set to conquer her body, mind and soul
Let him do as he pleases
Because that's the only way
She can be pleased too

Finally the moment draws near
The time is now!
Destiny is unfolding at last
She can hear
The galloping
Of his wild horse
She can hear his feet coming closer
Rapidly and without hesitation
Waiting even for a moment
Is now unbearable and painful!
She can feel his body next to hers
He is excited
He is going to do it
He is kneeling to kiss her
He is now kissing her with all his lust
She opens her eyes and smiles at him
He is determined, strong and brave
He is all over her
She cannot stop him
She doesn't want to stop him
The sleep is over
And the beginning
Of the greatest adventure of all
Begins—
The adventure
Of man and his woman
For right now
And for times to come

A Tale of Commitment

You have fallen for the Beast, Belle!
You love him with all your heart
He is very kind and he is also a real man—
He burns with endless lust
You cannot get enough of him!
You feel addictive to that terrific beast
What would your father and sisters say
If they knew who you are with?
Frankly that doesn't matter to you
They cannot provide
The love Beast feels for you
When you are in his arms, time stops:
He is strong like a rock mountain
He massages your soul endlessly
Until your moaning reaches heaven
There is nobody like him
So what he doesn't look hot?
He is definitely hot inside!

How can you leave him for few days
To see your dear dad and sisters?
It is hard to tell
Who will be missing whom more—
Beast or you, Belle?
You will be so miserable away from him
Even for just few hours
What if you cannot make it back on time?
What if something goes wrong?
You know your sisters can be mischievous
Yet you have to see your dad
Your dad is dying
You have no choice!
Besides, you do love Dad
Poor dad, he is lying in bed missing you!
Now that he sees you

He cries of joy
Why your sisters
Are more interested
In your clothes and jewelry
Than in you?
They even try to convince you
You should never to return to Beast
How dare they?
The more you stay in your father's house
The more you worry about Beast
You have to get back to him
He may be missing you
More than words can tell
He truly needs you
Like nobody else in the world
It is time to say "Goodbye"—
Kiss Dad
Kiss your sisters
And fly back

"Oh my God"!
Beast is lifeless!
How can that be?
You left ahead, not late
Poor Beast! He doesn't breath!
You heart is broken
For having broken
The heart of the guy who loves you
Tears run down your cheeks
You cannot stop crying
You realize now
You cannot live without Beast
Might as well you die too—
Life is not worth living without him
As your tears fall on Beast's eyelids
Beast awakens
And he becomes the prince he once was
Are you dreaming or is it really happening?

Beast is kissing you
And thanking you for saving him
He loves you with all is heart

A Tale of Compromise

You have turned
Into a lovely woman
Little Red!
Your mind and body
Are making you wrestles
Every day
It gets harder and harder
To deny yourself
What your heart desires
You are tired—
Of doing chores
And running errands
You want a place of your own to do it
And a guy to do it with
There are no guys your age
Living nearby
In the Land of Nowhere
What about the big bad wolf?
He is older and experienced
He is male all over
He knows what he is doing
He can give you a good time
He can be sweet and gentle
As you spread your wings
He can make you fly sky-high
You will treasure that first time
For years to come
You have to make a decision now
You won't be young forever
Do you want Mr. Right or Mr. Right-now?
Life can be unfair—
First we are cornered
Into a compromise
Later we have to put up
With a judgmental society

Should you save yourself
For that special guy if he exists?
Should you make yourself available
To the big bad wolf?
The wolf has had his eyes set on you
For a very long time
You know where to find him
He lives in the woods
He has one-track mind
Just like you, Little Red
When your grandma isn't around
You may use her place
Nobody needs to know
Only he and you—
Come on!
Do it!

A Tale of Compassion

They see the skin of the frog
But they fail to see the prince in you
You, Frog Prince, have been blessed
With a lot of love to give
But you have been cursed
With nobody to give it to
It is believed we have found true love
When our heart melts seeing
The one we love
Suffer and cry miserably
You have to find
That special someone
And melt her heart
She won't be able to resist
The fire that burns in you—
Overpowering
And intense

Hop, Frog Prince
Hop without getting stepped on
The road is treacherous
Full of obstacles and struggles
What other choice do you really have?
Live under the witch's spell
Or reach for the stars?
Please, don't cry!
Please believe in the impossible dream
The odds seem to be against you—
You feel you cannot go on
Your dream of true love
Will become a reality soon
Remember—
When all seems lost
And hope has deserted you
The miracle will happen

And the curse will be broken
She will find you
See you
And feel your anguish so much
Tears will appear in her eyes
She will, then, kiss you sweetly
To her own surprise and astonishment
The prince in you
Will come out of the frog skin
To kiss her back with joy!

A Tale of Hope

You need a break, Cindy!
Too much work for a sweet girl like you!
Life can be unfair—
Your stepsisters do nothing
While you do all the work
What makes it unbearable is
Nobody appreciates you
Not even a little
The magic of that first dance with the prince
You dream so much about
Seems just that
A sweet dream
That may never come true
It seems when we search for true love
We usually find disappointment
You cannot go on like this much longer!
Your fairy godmother wants to help you
She knows how, where and when
Will she help unleash
The true magic of love at first sight?
Will the prince be enchanted by you
As much as you are by him?

It is time, Cindy!
Wear the gown
Wear the glass slippers
Do it for your heart deserves
The very best in life!
Do it for those lonely people
Who will never experience real love

You have arrived at the ball
The music is enchanting and captivating.
You are afraid he will not notice you

Or like you
You are beautiful inside and outside!

You are the sun and the moon
You are the Morning Star
You deserve to be happy

Smile, Cindy, smile!
He has his eyes set on you
He cannot help it
He feels the anguish residing in your heart
He has experienced pain too
You feel his loneliness and his need
To make you his love and queen
He needs you as much as you need him
Can't you tell?
He is holding you in his arms
During the most beautiful dance of all—
The eternal Dance of Loving and Living
The dance of happy souls

You are looking into each other's eyes
And reading each other's thoughts
Dance, Baby Doll, dance!
Don't stop dancing!
Don't stop loving!
You have made it, Cindy!
Your wish upon a star
Has become reality

Fiber of Manhood

Soul of Man

The vision
The brave heart
The intelligence
The muscular physique
The sense of adventure
The masculinity
The superb looks
The innate charisma
The leadership
Walking with pride
The sexual prowess
Being right when—
Everyone else is wrong!
The interpersonal skills
The communication skills
It's getting up from a fall,
To walk straight and ahead,
To reach one's destination,
Untouched by hypocrisy!
It's accepting gladly God's will
By accepting the man within:
Body, mind, heart and soul!

Proud to Be Man

Proud to be mentally
And physically strong.
Proud to be daring
Without being reckless.
Proud to have character,
Courage, honesty and integrity.
Proud to be conscientious,
Tactful and also sensitive.
Proud to be confident
While striving to be a role model.
Proud to have common sense
And clear goals.
Proud to take charge, to make decisions,
To have a purpose.
Proud to be open-minded
And to know oneself.
Proud to have dreams and achieve them
With absolute determination.
Proud to accept one's limits,
Work out problems and never quit.

The Competition Drive

May the best man win!
Display your assertiveness
Show your aggressiveness
Show the brilliance of your mind

Let the right drive the wrong away
Let your masculinity
Drive you to fulfillment
Let your muscular physique
Help you lift burdens
Let vision and leadership
Guide you to success
Let compassion and temperance
Balance your life

Play smart, play hard,
Play safe or just play!
Be all you can be
Without forgetting who you are
Bend destiny to serve you
Without forgetting who helps you
Be the best you can be!
Win some; loose some.
Be the best man!

Man at Bat

It's spring!
A wake up call
To play baseball
The fans to enthrall
And there he is—
Man at bat!
He fixes his eyes on the ball
His spirit—ready for combat
The applause, the cheers and all
He hears not!
He is psyched—
Hears no sound!
Feels no pressure!
What really counts—
He and the ball

He got the full view
He's not going to miss
He is going the ball to crash
Only hitting, sliding and stealing exist
And the ball comes in a flash!

The sound of the hit—
A crack in the sky
He runs home
After he clears the bases!
He is the hero
And his team—his spirit
Now he hears
The applause and the cheers
Now he feels
The energy and the excitement
Of the team and the fans
Long live
Man at bat!
Hurrah!

Brave Heart

Alexander the Great
356-323 B.C.

Fathered in Macedonia by a king
Risen at sixteen to be himself king

Astute philosopher
    Unbeatable general
        Powerful king
Legendary personality
    A real man
        Almost a god!
A visionary
    With a mind driven
By unsurpassable bravery!

Conquered
    The civilized world of his days—
Such as Asia Minor
Spread Hellenism
    And founded Alexandria

At war—unbeatable
    In bed—passionate
He married
    And intermarried
At young age—
He was struck by a fatal fever
The world will never know
    Another Alexander the Great!

Man and Sinner
David
(2 Sam 11)

The look of lust is in your fascinated eyes.
You see Bathsheba through clothes—naked.
You're inflamed with passion, don't disguise!
Your masculinity wants to see her dominated.

She wants you too, David, and your male drive.
You got to have her; else you loose your mind.
She's hot, foxy and swiftly makes your lust thrive.
As flames consume you, your morality goes blind.

Reality wakes you up: you fathered her child.
So, first, you have her husband beguiled;
With a sword, then, you have him smitten.

The Valley of Shadow of Death through ridden,
You're sorry! You don't drink or eat, but weep.
You pray God in His infinite mercy—you to keep.

Vision and Skills

Teddy Roosevelt
1858-1919

Soldier then War Hero
Washington cowboy
Governor then President
Historian and explorer
Versatile statesman—
With Incredible energy
And distinctive masculinity

The Square Deal—
The handshake
Of the citizen
And the businessman
The Panama Canal successful negotiator
The Nobel Prize winner

The art of communication
Rooted in interpersonal skills
His charisma and lust for life
Left his image on Mount Rushmore
And in the hearts of many

Body and Soul

Extreme Wrestling
Jacob
(Gen 25-33)

Poor Jacob!
You are in serious trouble.
You pray God
To avoid what's inevitable:
Esau, your brother,
Is out there, you to assassinate.
You stole his birthright.
His anger now you must placate
You send him gifts—
Camels, goats and sheep
Doing your best,
May not assure your sleep.
You are truly scared.
You're surely trembling.
You see death
Quickly approaching.

Someone is behind you.
He calls you loudly by name.
He challenges you
To wrestle or it's your shame.
You got no time now for this.
He got you in a headlock.
You can't afford to be remiss.
You must fight and block.
Amazing!
Never before you felt this strong.
With him you wrestle all night long.
You win!
As the stranger departs,
He lands a kiss on your cheek;
Then he touches you on your thigh.

Suddenly in pain you shriek.
You're disabled and know not why.

The guy is no stranger, you've realized—
God Himself with you wrestled.
Let you win; yet left you disabled.
You got no time to consider this now.
Your family you get assembled,
Toward Esau limp in pain and plow.

Your brother,
You see from a distance.
He's strong.
He's set to advance.
When you get closer,
Esau's madness
As he sees you in pain,
Turns into sadness.
Down his face,
Tears are running.
His kid brother—limping!
Who were enemies previously
Are back on being siblings.

Unbelievable!
God with you fought
So you to be brave start.
He made you cripple
To soften Esau's heart.
You—a sinner
Who with God wrestles
A god who lets you
Cheat and win any less
A god who still saves
Your life regardless!

Fantastic Dreamer

Joseph
(Gen 37-50)

The Sun
The Moon
Eleven stars
And a sea of people
Will bow before you, Joseph!
Before your common sense
Before your intelligence
Before your sex appeal and fashion
Before yours, for Life passion
Before your sharp insight
Before your love of the Almighty

God has given you every opportunity
And every skill known to humanity—
You know everything
You can do anything
He has made you perfect by far
You are the beautiful Morning Star!
He has chosen your heart and mind
To dispense His love to mankind
Bring you will prosperity and shine
In a land troubled by war and famine
Shed you will light on the world
In the times ahead twirled

The road to greatness
Will be treacherous
And virtually crash you

Your brothers your doom will crave
And they will sell you off as a slave

You will be the target
Of desperate women
Who will, before you, kneel
So your charm and lust feel
You'll go to prison like a criminal
But with integrity you'll stand tall
You will sadly wonder along
What you have done so wrong
For God to act so toughly strong
If you look into your intellect, you'll err
In your heart you'll find the answer
You'll pass this horrific test
With your Faith and zest

The Pharaoh of Egypt, you'll sit by
He'll make you viceroy and his ally
Your sharp business skills
Will save the economy's ills
Pharaoh will care and love you a lot
For being his eyes, hands and heart
He will bear you sons
By one of his daughters
And to Jacob, your dear father—
You'll bring plenty of glory and honor

All generations to come
Shall forever call you blessed
And your deeds shall be praised
And truly blessed will be those
    Whose heart and life you'll touch

Sex for Money

The Sinful Woman
(Luke 7:36)

You wash His feet
With your profuse tears
And dry them
With your beautiful hair
In your heart—a silent prayer
Why can't you stop the tears?
Why are you crying so much?

God has bestowed
Upon you a lot of love
But no special guy
To share it with
You keep on crying
Because of a past
Of moral decadence
Wasted on men
And on false pretense

You see Jesus.
He's perfect!
He has a heavenly smile
The demeanor of a king
The bravery of a hero
Lots of wisdom
And a big heart
You cannot help but love Him blind
With all your heart, soul and mind
He is so perfect it hurts
But He'll never be yours
It's torture to see and touch
The one you love
You feel you're in a clutch—

He won't be yours ever
Your love is doomed forever
You wash His feet
With your profuse tears
And dry them
With your beautiful hair
Will this be enough for you,
Sweet Woman?
Will something
Be better than nothing?
Jesus smiles at you with warmness
And He says with kindness
"Your sins have been forgiven;
Your Faith has saved you!"

When your final day comes,
He will sweetly give you His arm
You'll enter heaven
And enjoy His charisma and charm
There—
Your struggle and anguish
Will be rewarded
And your heart—His Love
Will be awarded

Caught in Sin

The Adulteress
(John 7:53)

You've been hurled
On the ground—to be cruelly stoned
Your life flushes quickly
Before your eyes—you're astonished
You were once a young girl
Waiting for Love—you to twirl
Instead, your kisses were bought
By those same men,
Who have you now distraught
At present,
You've been caught in sin
Your fate has been sealed
Hopes and dreams
Have died long ago
You're ashamed
And feel terribly low
You have no strength
Or will to beg for mercy
You close your eyes
Oh, God, you regret it!
Your soul on and on cries
You cover your sad face
Silently you hope for grace
You wait for the first stone
The pain to swiftly erase
Cruelty and hypocrisy
Your sacrifice—are demanding
And your life are cruelly claiming

You hear someone
Addressing
The crowd in harsh tone:

"Let he, who is without sin,
Toss the first stone."

You raise your eyes
And see everyone—
Walk away in his or her sin
One by one

You're amazed!
You cannot believe
You look at Jesus
He says—
"Go and sin no more!"
As God's love and mercy pour
A new beginning
For you is finally in store
You get up shyly
And follow Him—humbly

May I, Sweet Lady,
Walk with you
On the road
To Redemption?

Epic Tale

Out of the darkness
Along came an evil knight
He rode a three-headed dragon
To destroy mankind
He had fire in his eyes
And war and pestilence
On his mind
He held a sword
Proven deadly
From ancient days
The breath of Death
Came out of his mouth
The knight rode the dragon
All over the sky
He disseminated destruction
Everywhere on land—
The middle head
Of the dragon spit fire
To burn pure love
The right head spit fire
To burn true passion
The left head spit fire
To burn dear possessions
This chaos made
Only room for—
Evil worship
Unclean passion
And dirty money
Old and young, men, women
And kids became slaves
Hope, Faith and Charity
Deserted Earth forever

A holy man was born
Out of a prayer recited

Over Moses' tomb
By few innocent kids
He was blood and flesh
He had wisdom
And a pure heart
He kneeled
Looked at the sky
And prayed for strength

Thunder and lightening filled the sky
And energized the holy man
The storm awoke Moses' shaft
Which landed in the hands of the Man

The holy man held the shaft tight
Pointed toward the dragon.
Lightening came out
And deadly hit the dragon
One by one
The dragon's heads
Rolled to the ground
The evil knight fell on his feet
Now he had to fight the old man
Face-to-face
Sword to shaft—
A fight that would determine
The future of mankind

It was a battle of wills—
The power of Good
Versus
The power of Evil

The fight intensified
As the two men were hitting
And hurting each other
Finally—the knight pierced

The old man's heart
With his sword

The old man
Hit the knight
With his shaft
At the touch of the shaft
The knight turned into stone;
Stone turned into fine sand
Sand turned into dust
The wind blew away
As the holy man closed his eyes
Welcoming Death
He became the prayer
That had given him life
A while before
The price of the battle
Had demanded a trade—
A life for a life
A personal sacrifice
For the greater good!

On the Road

How much love
Does our Heavenly Father
Bless us with?
So much
He turned
Adam and Eve's lost battle
Into the victory of Jesus
Over suffering and death

Celebrating Christmas
Means
Celebrating a birthday
That took place
Over two thousand years ago
God Himself,
Our Jesus,
Showed us
The perfect way
To live an enriching life—
The humility of a pure heart
Love for one another
And the acceptance of the Cross
Our personal cross
Is our road to heaven
Can we endure pain and anguish?
Yes, Jesus did
And so can we
Is it easy to turn suffering
Into an offering to God?
Only if we rely on God's strength
Because our strength
Is negligible

Every day
We face the challenge
Adam and Eve did—
We can have
Anything we want
Except one thing
It's a pretty good deal!

Christmas and Easter are
The pillars of a special love—
A love that goes far
And beyond
Human understanding
    Give
If you want to receive
    Love
If you want to be loved
    Forgive
If you want to be forgiven

We can join
The Cherubim and Seraphim
    Singing
"Glory to God
And Peace to all people
Of Good Will!"

Independence Day
July 4th, 1776

On the Mayflower, the Pilgrims bravely came
Seeking freedom from an oppressing land.
The people of thirteen colonies, holding hand,
Resented taxation without representation.

Like the people of other civilizations before,
They fought valiantly a revolutionary war.
On July 4th 1776, out of good men—a band
Signed the Declaration of a new free land.

On July 4th, 2007, 'cause of the flag, I fell off a ladder.
Hence I joined the wounded for not being wiser:
No foreign cannon ball or gun, I see and agree,
Can threaten a spirit determined to be free.

Exploring the Past

Sicily—the Land of Romance

An inviting smile on a beautiful morning
Can lead to a pleasant walk in the afternoon.
A pleasant walk on a lovely afternoon
Can lead to a sweet and tender kiss at midnight.
A sweet and tender kiss at midnight
Can lead to hugging and kissing all night long.
Hugging and kissing all night long
Can lead to heavy breathing and moaning.
Heavy breathing, moaning and longing for more
Can lead two bodies to become one flesh.
When two bodies become one flesh,
The earth trembles all over frantically,
The volcano shoots out its lava abundantly.
After the volcano shoots out its lava,
A sweet tender kiss can lead to another,
And to more hugging, kissing, moaning and loving.
The earth trembles all over frantically once more
And the volcano shoots out its lava again.
When a kid, your child, greets you with a hug,
Then you know the dream is dream no more.
You have been blessed from above
With a kind of love greater than yourselves.

Missing Sicily

As the ship away from land got farther and farther,
The pain in my agonizing heart felt like no other
A feeble voice inside expressed a sad complain—
The omen I would never see my Sicily again.

As the people, homes, buildings, streets and trees
Humbly like small and tiny aunts appeared,
My heart went into an unbearable painful squeeze.
My future mysteriously looked uncertain and feared.

Living in America as a successful family man
Feeling no longer a stranger in the brave land,
I long for enchanting Sicily where all began.

Going back on vacation is my dear plan.
On the Sicilian seashore I want lay and tan,
A prodigal son who to sweet home finally ran.

Sicilian Blood

I'm Sicilian and I'm proud!
Sicily is my mother—a sheer beauty!
The wind Sirocco, my father—pure fury!

What's in my blood is ancient history—
The Romans and the Greeks
Endowed me with no mystery—
The Arts and the Sciences!
The Saracens—the desire to explore
The Frenchmen and the Spaniards—
Lust for life, not just skills for war
Sicily—
      Land of agriculture
           And of fishery culture

The fertile Sicilian soil is in my blood—
The scenical Taormina
And the vibrant Tarantella
The Volcano Aetna and Mount Giuliano—very arena
The oranges, the lemons, the grapes
Olives, Tomatoes and wheat to exalt
Chestnuts, walnuts and pine seeds in all shapes
Sulfur, asphalt and plenty of salt

The Sicilian sky—
          The sun, the moon and the stars at night
The Sicilian seas—
Squid, octopus and muscles—health invite
Swordfish, tuna and the rainbow wrasse—are a might

Sicilian fire burns in my blood
   Yes, I am proud! Yes, I feel like a stud
I got the flair for my genes to bud

A Night Turned into Day

The night came before the final exams:
Apprehension, restlessness and insomnia.
So much to review and so much at stake!
The lights stayed on bright and unforgiving.
Page one turned to page two, and three,
And so on and on for a long time.
No time to rest, no time to sleep.
Just time to move on.
The night started to fly by very quickly.

What sunrise promised
Noon delivered.
The night that turned into day
Became a distant memory
Of young days—now long gone.

First Kiss

You and I share an unsinkable treasure.
We have the memories of what we felt,
We could've had, and we dreamed to have.

Love's first kiss uncovered
An exiting new world
We didn't know existed—
To have each other,
To be one flesh and one mind,
To experience happiness and pleasure
For the very first time.
We exchanged a special promise—
Always to be one mind, heart and soul.

As time passed
We enjoyed each other
Through our high school years.
Every day we made beautiful new memories.
Now that life is passing by, tell me, Baby,
You still remember that first kiss;
You still remember the magic we had;
You still remember
The gift of the love we shared.
We had it all—
True passion and real lust!

Remember our memories and dreams—
You know I always will.
I know you always will.

Sweetheart

Wonderful, lovely, a true sweetheart!
Yeager I was to be inside your very soul.
Heavenly, adorable and precious you were,
Eternal pillar of homely and sweet love.
Long last love from weary days,
Embracing you was all my heart desired.
Nourishing my soul with your kindness.
We abandoned ourselves to fairy tales.
Mine forever you were and I forever yours.
Yes, destiny bound us for a short time.
Love, when true, is supposed to last forever.
On eagle's wings, we rode to fulfillment,
Victory over loneliness and heartbreaks,
Everlasting seal on gentle souls.

First Fight

It was a real fight
With lots of nasty talk
It was a time
Of the turbulent teenage years

When I saw tears
Run down your face
I dropped on my knees
And hugged you at yours
My pain was unbearable—
Worse than agony and death
I hated myself
For what I had said

I never dreamed
Love could be so painful!
I was afraid to look up
And see you hurting
I wanted to tell you
How much I loved you
But I couldn't
I wanted you to hit me hard
Maybe to stop my suffering
Instead—
You walked away
Making me loose every hope

I found myself an inch away
From dying of broken heart
I had to be strong!
I had to confront you
I had to save the love
I didn't understand we had
I got up
Ran after you

And I yelled at you—
I would not allow you
To walk away from me
A miracle took place
You laughed
I laughed, too
Peace and serenity
Were restored in our little kingdom
It was a time of fig leaves bliss

Flipping a Quarter

You said I am passionate
As I am desperate.
I said you are wonderful
And full of sunshine.
You said there is more to me
That meet the eye.
I said you know I know
What makes you shine.
You said I tickle your imagination.
I said you bring out the best
And the worst in me.
You said it with a kiss on my cheek
And tears in your eyes.
I said it by holding you tight.
A quarter, that day,
Bought a piece of heaven.
I will always remember you, Mary Anne.
God bless you for shining
For me that special evening.

Candy Stripes

And there she was sweet Sheri
Among girlfriends—merry
At day in the sales arena,
In the evening a gentle ballerina

A dear girl with a broken heart
Needing a brand new start!
She had dreams that set her apart
She was charmingly smart.

Like all, she was at the club
At him—with wonders looking
He could be her dear hub
So she thought while drinking

He came close, in deed close,
Magic, poetry and prose!
Intensely against her, pressing—
Giggles, smiles, and sipping!

All leading to a perfect date,
Which turned out great.
Charmed, she swiftly ate the bait.
At night he was her mate.

In his fever—she sought pleasure
In her—he found treasure
Unleashed lust was his trait
For a while it was a kind fate!

Wild Within

I was once a cowboy
And you—
A wild mare!
You had no choice
But to close your eyes
And let it happen
You couldn't fight the feeling
    Endlessly lovemaking
Was all you desired
Breathtaking
You found
My drive to have you submit
To my pleasure
My two hands
Turned into a thousand
Feeling every inch
Of your body
You were a virgin
Very much in need
Of a real man
A man born to bust
Every lock of your doors
And to consume
The flames within you

I teased you to the edge of insanity
As my thumb snapped over your navel
You exploded in fireworks
Every time
I was inside your heart and soul
You squirmed
You twisted
You fought back

You reached the sky
Many times
I could see the colors
Of the rainbow
In your heavy breathing
And burning lust

Your moans
Driven by insatiable desire
Lead to indescribable pleasures
Pleasures
You had only dreamed of
And you had never
Experienced before
The rapture was indescribable!
You lived the moment
As to make it last forever
Reality and fantasy
Became one entity
You enjoyed it
You begged for more
        Feelings—
        Like love
        And the pain of longing
        The ecstasy
        Of an overheated encounter
        The misery of having to wait
        Until next time
        Happened all at the same time

Your secret fantasy
To be used
As a common harlot
Did come true that day

Your body ached for days
But the ecstasy you felt
Lasted forever

State of Sin

The Crisis

You are an old man and getting older!
You wake up in the morning with no job to go to.
You see yourself surrounded by problems:
    Insurmountable problems that won't go away.
God has abandoned you for a while
So your faith in Him may be tested.
The Devil will target you with fierce attacks.
You will suffer torment, wickedness and curses.
Satan will become you.
You will become Satan.
You will walk through the Valley
Of the Shadow of Death.
Only your faith might be your refuge.
What's wrong will appear right.
What's right will appear wrong.
What's important will appear unimportant.
What's unimportant will appear important.
People will see the smile on your face;
Yet Death will reside in your heart.
A sword will pierce your very soul.
Anguish will accompany your long days.

"In toils you shall eat all the days of your life.
Thorns and thistles shall grow for you.
By the sweat of your brow you shall eat your bread
Until you return to the ground because from it
You were taken. You are dust!
Into dust you shall return." (Genesis 3, 17)

Jesus will die on the cross for your sins.
You will be nailed on the cross next to Him.
"Because it is in giving that we receive.
It is in forgiving that we are forgiven.
It is in dying that we are born to eternal life"
(Saint Francis' Prayer)

The Devil's Promise

I make you a promise of—
Everlasting love,
Impressive sex,
And unlimited money.
You will get marriage proposals
By those whose heart
You'll touch and conquer.
You will master the ultimate intercourse—
Wrestling in bed, erotic massages,
Role-playing and lots of kinky stuff.
Slaves will offer you their mind
To serve and worship you.
They will also offer their soul
And body for your pleasure.
You will stretch their limits
And your own imagination.
You will bring to surface
Their subconscious fantasies.
You will dazzle and get money rewards.
Furthermore,
You will be admired,
Loved and appreciated.
You will grow powerful
In a powerless society.
You will wear only light
And easy to remove chains—
My reins to help you
Achieve your goals.
You don't have to do anything
You don't want to do.
We can stop at any time.
If you get hooked, it won't be the end—
Only the beginning
Of a real friendship
Between you and me.
No strings attached!
I promise you!

The Devil's Workshop

Say some truths
Say some lies

Once you get them confused
Strike them hard!

Say what they want to hear
Show what's good for you
Is even better for them

Sell the dream
Sell the fantasy
Show some care
Hold some back
Stretch their limits
Smile, charm and seduce

Let lust be your power tool
To bend their will
A notch at the time

You know you got them!
You know
You're the Master!

Unleashing the Alpha Male

Myth or reality?
Saint or sinner?
Healer or criminal?
Can one possess your body
And also your mind and soul?
Can one be a forceful lover
And, at the same time, a psychologist?
Can one break down the wall
Created by your self-defense mechanisms?

After Eve, born with a pure heart,
Ate the forbidden fruit,
Evil started to dwell in her—
Alongside her goodness.
The battle of Good versus Evil had been born
In the human heart.
The birth of the Alpha Male took place.
He has brute force of the mind
And kindness of the heart.
He gives humiliation,
And loving care as well.
He loves raw penetration, and also tenderness.
He can be the fruit of a creative mind
Or the fruit of a sick one.

Close your eyes to dream the impossible dream.
Wishes will be whispered in the dark.
Fantasies, residing in your mind,
Will become reality.
The senses, enhanced by mind control,
Will tease you until you reach ecstasy.
You shall hear songs never heard before:
Sweet words and rough talk, too.
Touching will highlight the magic
Where every inch of the body is explored.

You will taste real passion
And bring heaven down to earth.
You shall smell the scent of lovemaking
Behind the closed door of your lust.
You will look at the beauty in you
And feel perfect by being imperfect.
You shall have your limits stretched
While pleasure sets you free.
You shall please so you can be pleased.
You will give so you can receive.
It's a marriage of opposites—
It's Good and Evil, love and pain.

Imagine being free to be you!
No questions asked!
No explanations needed.
Let it be! Let it happen! Say "Yes"!

The Harlot's Soul

Surprised, she said, the harlot's soul?
Who does it for money,
Or has a heart of cold coal,
Or doesn't give honey.

Can the harlot's soul enhance life?
Give, take and withhold.
Be a lecher, also a sweet wife.
Titillate, tease and scold.

I believe in magic, I said.
Magic works with tricks.
Tricks may lead one to bed:
Chicks, licks and dicks.

There's much more to romance:
To go beyond the flesh;
To stretch limits and enhance;
To try the new and the fresh.

Have an image, homely and sweet.
Hide the wild libertine.
Turn the heat into a special treat.
Feed the man, but keep him lean.

Let's be vicious in innocence;
And innocent in vice.
Be daring, but apply prudence.
Always passion entice.

It's known the greatest biggest fool
Is who himself does fool.
What start as a mental exploration
Jeopardized holy salvation.

Master Training

You perform miracles, she said.
You are incredible!
With no you, I can't get ahead.
You are unbelievable!

Defensive like a dear father
On issues that matter.
Cheer and joy you scatter.
Inhibitions you shatter.

You're my God and my Lord.
The fancy becomes possible.
You're my dream and my reward;
Your savvy—shrewdly tribal.

For you I have immense respect.
You're sweetly amazing!
What's imperfect seems perfect.
You're heavenly inspiring!

Your help I need, my dear friend.
Surely, I did my best.
In your hands, I leave the rest.
My fiancé befriend.

Perform one more miracle.
Make my fiancé a master.
Make him lustfully satirical.
Do it fast; do it faster!

Cat and Mouse at Play

You are
An adventurous
Little mouse

I am a fat
Hungry
And shrewd
Big cat

You think you are so cool!
You think you are so hot!
You think you know it all
You think you can get away from me
Run all you want
Get through your head
You can't escape from me
You know
I know
You can't!
You're a player!
    I see it in your eyes
        I feel it in my heart
I am watching you
And the hole you live in
When I insert my paw into your hole
You hold your breath
And fight for your life
You cannot protect yourself from me
Your days are counted, Mouse!
I am going to make
A meal out of you
I am going
To love every minute of it!

The Sentry and the Gypsy

With his rifle erected
The sentry stands firm at the gate

The gipsy approaches
Glowing with smiles
Swinging her hips
She greets him
She gets close
Then very close
As her lips touch his
He grabs her
He lifts her up in the air
He foretells her future
His intense drive
    Will turn into an unstoppable frenzy—
    A fever born to consume
    Her mind and soul
    A passion meant
    To become her addiction
    A force that will turn her
    Into his pleasure slave

    She is going—
To give in
Bend to his will
Please him
In every possible way
Worship him as her god
She won't be able
To stop him
Or refuse him anything
He will become
Her only reason to live
She—his pleasure machine

She accepts her fate
He delivers
What he has foretold her

The Cop and the Habitué

In the dark alley
The cop throws
The habitué against the wall
He makes her spread out
Her arms and legs
The situation is hopeless!
She has broken the law
One too many times.
He frisks her—
Finds no weapon
Or illegal substances
He calls her names
He is fed up with her behavior
He presses himself against her back
The spirits of the savage within
Take over
She sighs in anguish
She moans with longing in her heart
He becomes a wild beast
He cannot stop
Even when he wants to
His hands massage her very soul
He smacks
    He spanks
        He shouts
            He curses
She realizes now he is no ordinary man
He is the Man!
The mind of a rugged man
The soul of a forceful man
The roughness of an unyielding man
The intoxicating language
Of a true master
He is powerful
    He is severe

He is virtually unbeatable
He is Draconian!

As pleasure lubricates her soul
She let go a cry
In the mist of his rapture
He squeezes her skintight
She can feel
His discharge inside
Drowning her in ecstasy

The Master and the Succubus

Enters
The Master
Down the sharp cellar staircase
He swaggers
Intoxicated with anger
He curses at the succubus.
She is caged
She curses her fate
He reaches the cage
He looks at her with his piercing eyes
She understands he is in control
He is the ultimate Alpha Male—
Her very reason to fulfill her destiny

She kneels
She makes no sound
He opens the cage
She steps out
She lays flat on her stomach before him
He cracks the whip and hits her
She jumps on him
He grabs her neck with both hands
And forces her down on her knees
So she can pleases him
He grabs her head
Forces her to open her mouth
He goes deep into her very soul
Now docile
She fulfills her duties
And her mission in life—
To please herself
Only by pleasing
Her potent Master

He reaches deeper inside her

She is under his control
Of the majestic and might mind,
Of her powerful and unyielding man
Her feelings to give pleasure are inebriating
She hugs his back
She feels her magic spot
Only for her heart
To explode in rapture
Firm, bold and rugged
He shouts and curses
As he reaches ecstasy

She gets locked back into her cage
To serve him later

The Price of Sin

As the eyes in oblivion closed,
The Garden of Eden appeared.
It meant to become kids again—
Exploring was the goal to attain:
No inhibitions, no thinking,
Only craving for gratification.
As the clothes came off frantically,
The mind was freed to explore.
Heavy petting, was the air painting
With the colors of the rainbow.
Hands could feel the soul aching
With the desire to explode.
The bottomless pit of gratification
Couldn't be reached within human means.
Lust became a rampant addiction
After the heart grew wrestles in sin.

The Serpent,
The uncanniest of all animals,
Empowered seduction:
Knowledge and skills of ancient times
Dazzled and excited the mind.
Suddenly the Garden of Eden bloomed
With every imaginable flower and fruit.
The angels filled the air with their melody
"If you eat the fruit, you shall die".
Adam and Eve awoke
Only to fail miserably
By repeating their sin.
The Serpent bit the human flesh
With its lethal discharge.
Genesis had come alive again
As the battle
Of Good versus Evil
Continued.

Fatal Demise

You truly had it all, Lucifer, only to loose it all.
The Almighty created you, to glow and to shine.
To charm and to give was simply your call.
Then Ego came—and nothing again was ever fine.

Why not receive happiness at least for a change?
Why just live a life of giving without receiving?
You willingly lead others and yourself into derange,
Instead of running away from sin and flings.

You defeated the very reason behind your creation,
You stopped shining and glowing; you fell into hell.
Now you immensely hated yourself and every nation.

Lasting doom became your painful place to dwell.
Over time, into pure evil, your hate finally bloomed.
Guess now, Lucifer, who else Ego consumed?

Funky Therapy

The Fall

As the ladder gave in,
I landed in the kingdom
Of pain and regrets

Cursed be the ladder that lead me
To a horrible and atrocious fall!

I found myself crucified next to Jesus
Just like the two thieves so long ago
"Will you, Sweet Jesus, remember me
When you enter your kingdom"?
I desperately wanted to hear Jesus say
"This very night you will be with me"
Instead a choice
Was laid before me
In a dream—
Either you join the eternal dance
   In the heavenly sunny prairie
Or you accept Life
With all its
Overwhelming
Problems
The choice was Life
For the love of my family!

Now feeling—
Worn out
Shaken up
And beaten
I hang out with my new friends—
Pain
Discomfort
And misery
I offer
The Almighty God

The fruits of my suffering—
Heart-felt compassion
   For the sick and the hurt

The Psychiatrist

Let's talk about depression!

When your hopes and dreams
Have been crushed
When loneliness and adversity
Reign supreme in your life
When the smile is gone, never to return
When tomorrow has lost its entire luster
When anticipation has been dead for years
When the birds sing for everyone else
When the flowers don't bloom for you
When the day is very long
And the night is very short
When all seems fine on the outside
But it is hell inside,
When you look in the mirror
And Death looks back at you,
When you just wait for your fate
To complete its painful course

The Psychologist

Lets talk about loneliness!

Loneliness—perfidious venom!
On things made of dreams,
Never told or spoken swiftly,
Eager with enthusiasm and full of hope,
Love elusive, yet appealing,
I inhaled the fire of lust for life.
Never one to understand me around,
Everlasting pervasive sadness bound,
Sent me on a journey of introspection,
Set to discover the hero in me.

The Physical Therapist

…And God created Peter the Therapist
Out of gold dust and foamy seawater
The Almighty made him
Lean, mean and tough on pain
Our Heavenly Father gave him—
A killer smile
Healing hands
Lots of energy
Lust for life
And enthusiasm.

He is dashing and forceful
Savvy and understanding
Results oriented and humorous
He has a business mind
And a heart of gold

God gave Peter the Rock a mission:
To take the good people—
Out of the bondage
Of pain and sorrows
Into the prosperous kingdom
Of Loving and Living

He's family!
He's a friend!
He's a healer!

He is the Physical Therapist!

The Occupational Therapist

On a mission to heal the injured or ailing hand,
The Almighty sends lovely Judie to massage,
Bend, stretch, twist, exercise and comprehend,
Though recovery seems an illusion or a mirage.

Like her Biblical persona, with perseverance she fights
The bureaucratic system on behalf of the sick or hurt,
By changing eagerly with passion wrongs into rights.
She's smart and sweet, caring, sensitive and alert.

The healing process can be very slow and daunting,
Scary, overwhelming, frustrating and discouraging.
She applies expertise, wisdom, patience and fine tools.

Hope, Faith and Charity are her enchanting jewels.
Even though accidents and malaise seem to abound
She brings comfort and joy by just being around.

The Priest

You act like a good and loving guy
But are you?
Do you take more than you give
Or vice versa?
Do you put others first?
Are you aware
Of the people around you
Who need you
Sometimes badly?

If you live your life
To please yourself
Then your heart is made of stone
You are virtually—
Indifferent
And insensitive
To others' needs

You were born—
    To rise above chaos
            Problems
                    And mediocrity
To reach for the stars
To touch the hand of the Almighty
Only then, God can give you
His love for you to share it
With your brothers and sisters in Christ
And to find peace within yourself

Are you man enough
And tough enough
To sacrifice yourself for others?
Once you agree
There will be
No more you as you know it

But a new you
A better you
A happier you
A holy and just man
Our Lord does great things
With those who have a pure heart—
Your heart will burn
With the flame of true love
Your eyes will finally bear tears
You will walk tall
On the road to Redemption

You have to give generously
If you want to receive abundantly
You have to swallow your pride
And yet smile with serenity
You have to die to yourself
So you can be born
To a spiritually fulfilling life

You will feel like the bright Morning Star
Shining over the people around you
Sharing Love, Faith and Hope

Home Joys

The Little Flower of Lubacaw

In the heat of intense passion forged,
Honey and berries feeding,
The Little Flower of Lubacaw bloomed
Into the Goddess of Hunting.

The ancient Evil Dragon confronting
She flew up in the sky
Bravely with bow and arrows packing,
Her skills and wit to apply.

The fighting grew viciously intense.
With the dragon's killing,
The battle was no longer suspense.
Her future was smiling.

After the wrongs turned into rights,
Tales told and divulged.
Peace ruled the days and nights.
The people serenely indulged.

Gems crowned her pretty head
At Love's first kiss.
The petals of white flowers lead
To a fairy tale bliss.

There she stood as my darling wife
In the Holy Tower,
Lovely Diane, the love of my life,
My Little Flower of Lubacaw.

Love in the Elevator

In the old elevator we were delightfully stuck.
One on top of the other, sweetly and snugly tuck.
A precious moment that was never forgotten!
A fast heartbeat and pure lust had us gotten.

A time for sweet memories and unleashed passion:
It was raw romance without any pretense!
Hopes and dreams were definitely in our fashion.
No common sense, but the fire was quite intense!

Under the holy blessings of a devoted Christendom,
Our life together, with time, bloomed into stardom:
An enchanted marriage of souls and fruitful parenthood.

The youth of the heart is surely ours for good.
The youth of the face now faintly fades;
But delightful memories will come in many shades!

Marriage Bliss

Happiness arrived when I first met you.
I have you forever to hold and to cherish.
Pressing my body against yours has unleashed
Torrents of flames and sublime passion.
I believe in a sun that never sets.
I believe in you and me in Wonderland!
I only dreamed magic would visit my lonely heart;
But I have entered the palace of enduring love,
Excited by enjoying your mind, body and soul.

Last day will never come
Because our love lasts forever.
When old, embracing and longing for more,
Our lips will still tremble at the touch
Until dawn wakes us up
In the Heavenly Kingdom.

Thank you, Diane, for giving me
The greatest gift of all—
The gift of true love!

My Wife and Queen

Spellbound I'm by a rare enchantress,
Smart, sexy and alluring!
The pair of hazel eyes of a seductress
A smile—glowing and captivating

In church I stood in festive style,
Happy to see you delighted
Walking up along the flowered aisle
As a veiled bride—excited!

A secret door leading to heaven
Is your womanhood's leaven.
When motherhood became you,
To touch the sky, I flew.

Even though struggles and sorrows
May scar a pure heart,
Them away, your sharp ingenuity blows.
Our love won't depart!

As the flames of love and passion explode,
We travel afar.
With all the great gifts on me bestowed,
You're my shining star.

Listen to your gentle and dear heart.
To me, walk toward.
I—perfect by being humanly imperfect!
You—my precious reward!

Of Memories and Renewed Vows

What makes you, Diane, my special princess?
Your starry eyes—
Your inner beauty
Your pure heart
Your heavenly smile

When I met you, I was spellbound by—
Your personality
Your looks
That enchanting turquoise
Flowery sleeveless
Mini-dress you were wearing
I was never the same!
My search
For the perfect girl and soul mate
Was finally over!

True love
Tested by time
Has taken us far beyond
Virtually insurmountable obstacles

Even though I don't deserve you
I cannot help falling in love with you over again.

I cannot get enough of you!
I want you every minute
Of every day and every night
I love you
With all my heart and soul
I want to cherish you
In this life and in the next

I take you again for—
My partner in life
My true and only love

Thank you, Diane,
For all you have given me

Thank you
For letting me believe
In myself again

What's a Son?

He's your very own blood and flesh!
First, he brings baseball trophies,
Later, girlfriends—foxy and fresh.
Ambitions are his life philosophies.

What's a son? Your very champion!
He makes you feel king of the castle
And the leader of a fabulous nation.
He fights your battles without hassle.

He has your lust for life and flair.
He is the answer to your prayer.
The miracle father and son share!

On your lap he'll place a grandchild.
For posterity your name will be styled.
You'll smile with your heart delighted.

Paternal Magic

I say it
You hear it
I charge
You wait
I wonder
You smile
I get upset
You stay cool
But –
When opportunity knocks
You already know what to do
That's the magic
Between
Father and son

Brave as a Knight, David

Born as a dashing and daring knight,
You made your entrance into the world,
On a cold and snowy February night.
With happiness, mom and dad swirled.

You played as a pleasant boy would;
But didn't study as a good boy could.
Toys and clothes for you we bought.
Trophies and friends, home you brought.

Always loving sports, fun and action,
Funky speedy wheels are still an attraction.
Grown into a fine man you have now.

With skills and wit, at work you plow.
You face the challenges of a real man.
Battle and win like nobody else can.

A Heart of a Son—Mark

Goodness in your heart reigns supreme.
Love and lust for life your days inhabit.
You can make the sun at night gleam.
Lying back to daydream you make a habit.

Joking, laughing or just fooling around,
Time passes by without making a sound.
You know more tricks than a magician.
Use your art and craft to fulfill ambition.

The day will come you will find Love
Choose wisely; yet follow your heart.
Be very sure she fits you like a glove.

To fulfill dreams, work hard but smart.
Remember to look inside for the answer
And also trust in God, our Lord to confer.

A Comedian in a Son—Daniel

When sad and melancholy, I think of you.
I recall yours jokes and I'm no longer blue.
Your voice mail greetings make me laugh:
Plenty of humor in everyone's behalf.

A student, a body builder and a handy man!
Busy you keep yourself from dawn to dusk.
Nothing too small or too big: all you can!
Versatile in cooking: pasta, meats and rusk.

You're a bit of genius and also my hero.
You make money, but in the bank it's zero,
And can't believe you drive on old wheels.

A hand therapist, too: stretches and bends.
Sympathetic to pain; you know how it feels.
Smart you are to cherish good old friends.

Future Grandson

Very long ago
At the beginning of times
Your name was written
In the Book of Life
By our Loving and Merciful God
Your coming has been foretold
In my dreams and in the cards

Your great-grandparents
And great-great grandparents
Suffered the atrocities
Of two World Wars
So I could come to the Land of the Brave
To become your grandfather

I left family and friends behind
What I didn't leave behind or gave up
God took it away from me anyway
But He gives me you
For my heart and soul
You and I will be one mind
In the service of God and the country
We will be very close
And fond of each other

You will live in difficult and trying times
Where civil unrest
Will plague every land
You will have to look into your pure heart
To find solutions
To virtually impossible problems

When your need
For comfort and moral support
Seem overwhelming

Visit me!

My spirit will be there for you in church,
Next to the candle flickering the most

You will win over adversities
And help restore prosperity
Many will love you
And admire
Your courage
And determination

Your name shall glitter
In glory and splendor
Even after
You will be long gone

In good or bad times
Here on Earth or in heaven
I will always love you, Grandson